KT-116-197

GERVELIE'S JOURNEY

A Refugee Diary

Anthony Robinson

and

Annemarie Young

Illustrated by June Allan

F

FRANCES LINCOLN
CHILDREN'S BOOKS

This is the true story of Gervelie's journey, told in her own words. It follows her from her home in the Republic of Congo, to the Ivory Coast, Ghana, across Europe and on to England where she now lives with her dad, Gervais.

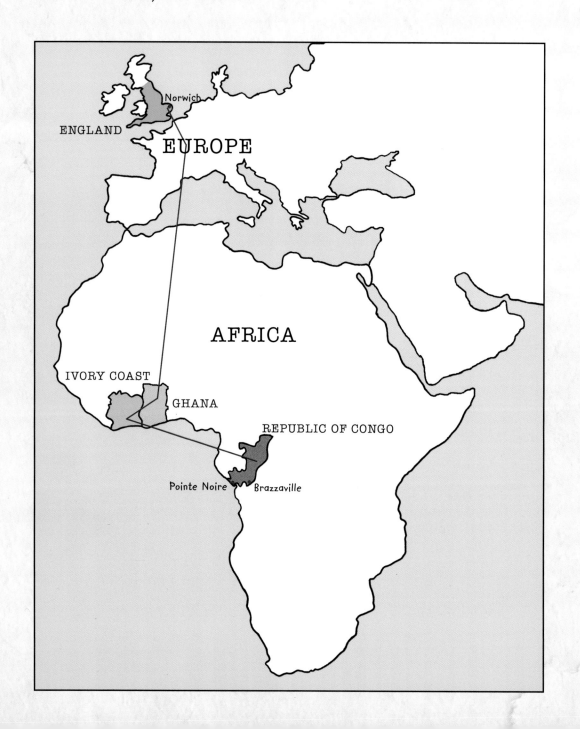

This book is to be returned on or before
the last date stamped below.

acher.

He has liv   ome in Australia
to Southeast   ives in Cambridge.
He is par   children's lives,
be they re   ing normal lives
in va   cumstances.

ANN   consultant.
She has liv   ome in Australia
to   mbridge.
She l   citing ideas,

JU   drawing.
                                                                  m!

She at   as a teacher,
then as   children's book
ill   's books.

LIBREX

Education
Library
Service

CLASS NO:

325.21

3 1 JAN 2011

ildren,

This book is dedicated to Gervelie and Gervais,
and to all those who are struggling to be free.

The Authors would like to thank Joanna Snape and the Red Cross
in Norwich for introducing them to Gervelie and Gervais.

This is a picture of me

My name is Gervelie. I was born in 1995 in Brazzaville, the capital of the Republic of Congo. I lived with my mum and dad in the south part, in a nice house in the suburb of Moukondo. My dad's mum, my auntie and uncle and cousin lived nearby. Dad worked as a travel agent and Mum stayed at home.

I was two when the trouble started. My dad has told me what happened. I ask him all sorts of questions and he gives me answers when he can.

Brazzaville, Republic of Congo, 1997

The trouble started in Brazzaville in June, 1997.
When the Cobra militia attacked the area where
we were living, we had to get out very quickly
because it was just too dangerous.

It was chaos. Everybody was trying to get away.
I went with my grandma to a safer part of the city.
Dad was looking for Mum. He spent two weeks looking
for her. He looked everywhere, and in the end he gave
up. It was very dangerous for him to be in Brazzaville
but Dad was worried about Mum. Later we found out
that she had gone to stay with relatives.

After a few weeks, when it was quieter, Dad and I got out.
We took a minibus and then a plane to Pointe Noire, on
the coast, so Dad could find work. My grandma went to
the Ivory Coast because she owned a house there.

Pointe Noire, Republic of Congo, 1999

We stayed in Pointe Noire until 1999, when I was about four.
Some of Dad's friends warned him that bad people were
looking for him. Then a terrible thing happened. Some men
came to his father's house looking for Dad. A cousin who
was there panicked and ran away. As he was trying to get
over a wall they shot and killed him. My granddad tried
to stop them so they shot him too. His neighbours took him
to hospital, but he died. Dad was so sad.

Dad fled to the Ivory Coast to stay with my grandma,
and Mum came and got me and took me back to Brazzaville
to live with her. She was now married to a Police Commander
so she thought I would be safer with her.

Brazzaville, Republic of Congo, 1999

I hated being separated from Dad but at least I was with my mum. Even speaking to Dad on the phone was difficult and dangerous for Mum. I didn't see Dad for a whole year, and I was beginning to forget what he looked like.

It was the worst year of my life. My stepdad beat me. He would hit me with the buckle of his belt. There were always guns in the house and my stepdad once nearly killed a man in front of me. I saw things – horrible things. My stepdad was a very powerful and dangerous man and Mum could not protect me. I really wanted my dad then, but what could I do?

One day my grandma came to visit. Dad had asked Grandma to come and take me away to live with her in the Ivory Coast. Mum wouldn't let me say goodbye to my little half-sister. She said my sister would want to come with me. Mum packed a few clothes for me, and then I left with Grandma. I would've just liked to say goodbye to my little sister and my friends.

This is my little sister

Ivory Coast, 1999

I was very happy with Grandma. Dad worked far away. Then he started visiting. The first time I saw him, I didn't recognise him. His face had changed or something. But then it was fine. He visited me a lot after that and sometimes took me away for the weekend. I still missed my mum, but not the other things in Brazzaville. It was good to feel safe.

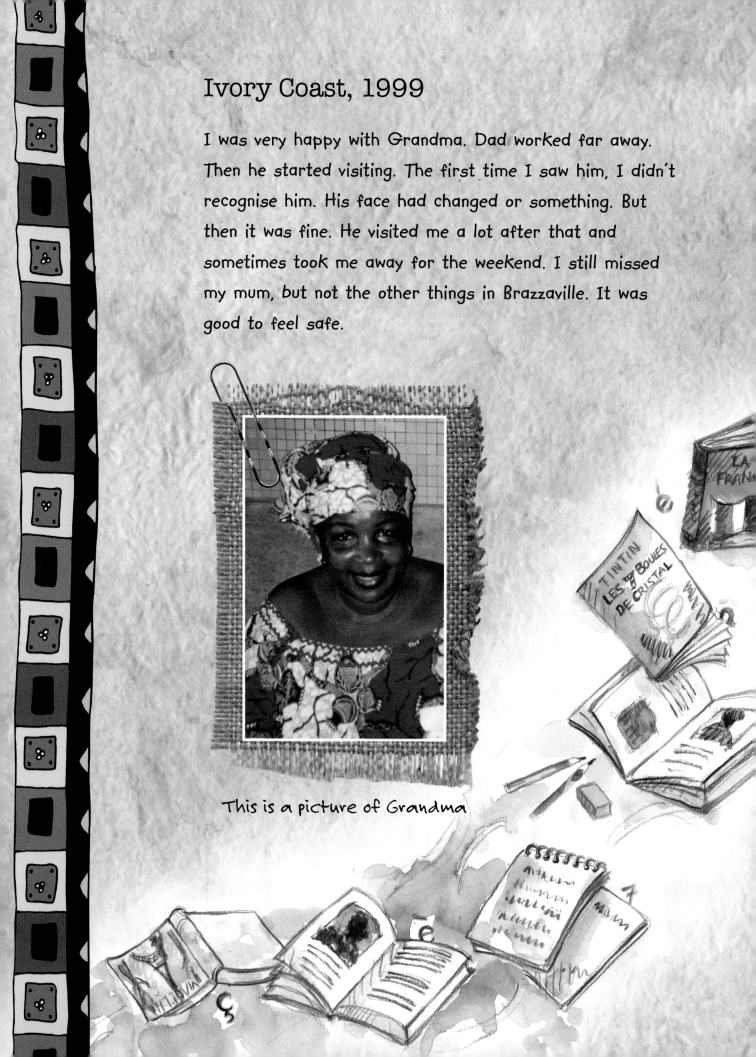

This is a picture of Grandma

This is a picture of me when
I was living in the Ivory Coast

I went to school by bus in the Ivory Coast.
The lessons were in French, which was OK because
I spoke French in Brazzaville. I loved being at school
and learning, but the teachers were very strict.
Wednesday was a free day, but you could go in for
extra lessons if you wanted, and I always did. Finally,
everything seemed to be going well for Dad and me.

Ivory Coast, 2001

Then in 2001 a war started in the Ivory Coast.
Sometimes I think we are really unlucky!

We couldn't go back to the Congo and everybody we knew
was leaving the Ivory Coast. It was no longer safe
to live there. You could be shot if you were outside at the
wrong time. If the soldiers asked a man to join them, they
would kill him if he refused. There were guns everywhere
and shooting all the time. I was terrified of anyone wearing
a uniform. So Dad and I decided that we should escape
to Europe.

Europe, 2002

We left the Ivory Coast in December 2002. I thought we
would go by train and I don't like trains – two of my uncles
were killed in a train attack. But we flew in an aeroplane.
I don't remember much about the journey. I slept most of
the time. We landed in Ghana, which was OK. No trouble.

We caught another plane and flew to Europe. We stayed with
some cousins who lived there. I can't tell you which country
it was because we were not supposed to be there and our
cousins would get into big trouble if the government found out
they had helped us. It was Christmas and it was very cold.
I had never been cold before. Grandma had put some
jumpers in my suitcase and I was glad of that.

Celebrating my 7th birthday

I celebrated my 7th birthday there. I didn't get
a call from Mum or a card, even though she knew
where we were.

Dad couldn't get a visa for us to go to France, but
we got some borrowed documents to go to England
instead. Moving. Moving. Always moving.

Luton, England, 2003

We left for England in March 2003. Dad told me we had 'special' documents. We had to use other peoples' names to travel to England, so we had to destroy these papers as soon as we got on the plane, to protect the people who had lent us their names.

We arrived at the plane station in Luton, in England, on 31st March, without any documents. Dad immediately asked for asylum. We were both very, very scared when we got to Immigration Control.

We were interviewed by Immigration Officers. One really upset me because he shouted at Dad, "You're lying! You're lying! Tell me the truth!" I hid behind Dad. This man was African, like us, but he was really horrible.

Then we were put in a taxi. Nobody told us where we were going, not even the interpreter. My dad was really worried about money for the taxi. All through the three-hour taxi ride he was worried about how he would pay.

We were going to Ipswich, we just didn't know it. Dad nearly cried when he realised the taxi was already paid for. And they were expecting us at the hotel and told us the hotel was paid for too. Dad was so relieved. Why didn't they just tell us?

Ipswich, England, 2003

The next day we had a meeting with the Refugee Council. This was much better for Dad. They had a French speaker and Dad asked a lot of questions for the first time. I could mostly understand what they were talking about.

The food in the hotel was OK, but always the same. Breakfast was Weetabix and milk. That was strange for me. Lunch was usually fish and chips, and dinner was chicken and chips. Everything and chips. We didn't have rice, and I really missed that.

But we made church friends in Ipswich. That's where we met one of my godmothers, Stella. The Refugee Council also found me a school, Springfield Junior. It was great. They gave me a special friend too. Her name was Chelsea. We couldn't speak English together, but it was nice to have a friend.

After a little while the Refugee Council found us a hostel. Dad was doing some volunteer work for the Refugee Council. Sometimes I was in the house alone all day. I didn't like that at all.

And then it happened again. We had to leave. No time to say goodbye to our friends. Dad came to school and said he had got a letter and we had to leave that afternoon. Just like that. It made me sad, like when I had to leave my little half-sister in the Congo. We were being sent to Norwich.

Port Reference:
Home Office Reference:
UK IMMIGRATION SERVICE
LONDON LUTON AIRPORT,
LUTON, BEDS, LU2 9LU

Fax: 01582 405215

01582 439030

ON OF TEMPORARY
TO BE DETAINED

admission to the United Kingdom subjec

POSTAGE PAID

GREAT BRITAIN

ON OFFICER

Norwich, England, 2003 – 2004

In Norwich we were given our own house and the Refugee Council gave us some money. The first thing we did was go to the supermarket and get some food. We bought meat and vegetables and went home and cooked our first meal together. It was great.

Dad cooking a meal

We made good friends in Norwich – mainly through our church. Stella's friend from Norwich, Isabel, came to see us, and later I met Barbara, who became my godmother. I was baptised in March 2004. A month later I had my First Holy Communion. We had a party and Stella came from Ipswich. So I had two godmothers. It was a good time for me and Dad.

Me and Dad at my First Communion
with Isabel, Stella and Barbara

Me and my Norwich friends in our street

Norwich, England, 2004 – present

In September I started at St Thomas More School.
That was Year 4. I'm now in Year 8. I really like school here.
They don't beat you if you make a mistake, and they explain
things better too. And I love all the books I can get here.
I love reading. I like scary stories the best. My dad laughs
and says, "Haven't you been scared enough, Gervelie?" and
I think, well I can close the book if I want. I couldn't close
the book in Africa, or in Luton, or in Brazzaville with
my stepdad.

Me in my school uniform

We get sad sometimes when we miss Africa and my mum.
If Dad gets cross with me I miss Mum a lot and I go to my
room and take out pictures of her. Sometimes I cry. I think
of my little half-sister too.

I love my mum, even if she's not there when I need her.
She hasn't called for a long time, and I get upset if she
doesn't call on my birthday. My dad's the only one who has
ever said, 'Happy Birthday'. Dad thinks that ringing us might
be difficult for her. I don't know. Mostly Dad and I are OK
here. Except in February, when he remembers his dad's
murder. It's hard to celebrate my birthday then.

We feel safe here, but we don't know yet if we will be able
to stay. We have friends and I have Barbara. But she's not
my mum, is she?

The Future

I would like to be a lawyer or a singer one day. I wanted to be a teacher when I was younger. I love learning things. I love singing in church, at home and at school. I really enjoy music, especially R'n'B. Reading and music are my favourite hobbies.

Dad and me at home

Some days I think I would like to go back to Africa when I'm older. Other days I want to stay here. I don't know. It's confusing. Now we are just waiting to see if we can stay in England. I don't want to move around any more. Someday I hope to go to America. Not at the moment. I want to make new friends, learn more things and I want Dad and me to always feel safe.

Did you know?

★   The Republic of Congo is a West-Central African country. It borders Gabon, Cameroon, the Central African Republic, the Democratic Republic of Congo, Angola and the Gulf of Guinea.

★   It covers an area of 342,000 square kilometres (over 152,000 square miles).

★   The capital city is Brazzaville.

★   The longest river is the Congo.

★   About 4 million people live in the Republic of Congo.

★   The people speak French, Lingala, Monokutuba and Kikongo.

★   In the 1880s, it became a French colony. It gained its independence from France in 1960.

What happened?

The recent history of the Republic of Congo is very complex, and this is just a brief outline.

In 1992 Pascal Lissouba became the country's first democratically-elected President. Soon after this first election, in 1993, fighting broke out between government forces and the opposition, who had disagreed with the election result. The fighting continued until 1995 when both sides agreed to stop. Peace continued until just before the next elections, which were due in July 1997.

On 5 June 1997, trouble began between the government forces and the Cobra militia. This was the beginning of five months of terrible fighting. The result was that Brazzaville was almost totally destroyed, and tens of thousands of men, women and children were killed. This is what Gervelie and her family fled from.

Since the publication of this book, Gervelie and her father
have been granted asylum in the UK.

GERVELIE'S JOURNEY copyright © Frances Lincoln Limited 2008
Text copyright © Anthony Robinson and Annemarie Young 2008
Illustrations copyright © June Allan 2008

First published in Great Britain and in the USA in 2008 by
Frances Lincoln Children's Books, 4 Torriano Mews,
Torriano Avenue, London NW5 2RZ
www.franceslincoln.com

First paperback edition published in Great Britain in 2009
and in the USA in 2010

All rights reserved

No part of this publication may be reproduced, stored in a retrieval system,
or transmitted, in any form, or by any means, electrical, mechanical, photocopying,
recording or otherwise without the prior written permission of the publisher
or a licence permitting restricted copying. In the United Kingdom such licences
are issued by the Copyright Licensing Agency, Saffron House,
6-10 Kirby Street, London EC1N 8TS.

British Library Cataloguing in Publication Data available on request

ISBN 978-1-84780-004-6

The illustrations for this book are in watercolour

Printed in Singapore by Craft Print Int'l Ltd. in March 2010

3 5 7 9 8 6 4 2

MORE PAPERBACKS FROM
FRANCES LINCOLN CHILDREN'S BOOKS

Home Now
Lesley Beake
Illustrated by Karin Littlewood

How can Sieta feel happy with so many sad pictures inside her head? She remembers her real home far away over the mountains, her parents getting sick and Aunty taking her to live in a place she calls Home Now. Home Now is full of people building new houses and new lives. They smile at Sieta, but Sieta can't smile back – until one day her teacher takes her class to the elephant park. There Sieta meets another orphan with memories like her own.

The Colour of Home
Mary Hoffman
Illustrated by Karin Littlewood

Hassan feels out of place in a new cold, grey country. At school, he paints a picture showing his colourful Somalian home, covered with the harsh colours of war from which his family has fled. He tells his teacher about their voyage from Mogadishu to Mombasa, then to the refugee camp and on to England. But gradually things change. When Hassan's parents put up his next picture on the wall, Hassan notices the maroon prayer mat, a bright green cushion and his sister Naima's pink dress – the new colours of home.

Petar's Song
Pratima Mitchell
Illustrated by Caroline Binch

Petar loves music, and his violin keeps the whole village dancing. But when war breaks out, Petar, his mother and his brother have to leave the valley and flee across the border to safety, leaving their beloved father in the village with the other men. Petar is so sad that he can no longer play his music – until one day a song of peace, spring and new beginnings starts to form in his head…

Frances Lincoln titles are available from all good bookshops.
You can also buy books and find out more about your favourite titles,
authors and illustrators on our website: www.franceslincoln.com